JOAN OF ARC

The Maid of Orléans

Written by Benoît-J. Pédretti
Translated by Jessica Foster

History   50MINUTES.com

50MINUTES.com

BECOME AN EXPERT
IN HISTORY

George Washington

The Battle of Austerlitz

Neil Armstrong

The Six-Day War

The Fall of Constantinople

www.50minutes.com

JOAN OF ARC

KEY INFORMATION

- **Born:** 1412, in Domrémy (Kingdom of France).
- **Died:** 30 May 1431 in Rouen (Kingdom of England).
- **Main achievements:**
  - In the early 15th century, a young peasant girl from the eastern outer edges of the Kingdom of France made a name for herself with the French people: she stated that she carried a divine message that required her to liberate France. The country was, in fact, partly in the hands of the English and the Burgundians. Charles VII (1403-1461), the legitimate heir and successor to the late Charles VI (1380-1422), had not yet been crowned.
  - Whether truly a prophet or a fraud, she managed to persuade the heir apparent to entrust a small troop of soldiers to her to fight the English, and won some astounding victories. She recaptured Orléans at the beginning of May 1429. With enthusiastic public support, she had many successes in battle and eventually led Charles to Reims, where he was crowned king of France on 17 July 1429.
  - Shortly afterwards, she was wounded, captured and sold to the English. Her fate was sealed. In Rouen, which was in English territory, Pierre Cauchon (1371-1442), the bishop of Beauvais, brought a resounding case against her in court in the spring of 1431. Joan was sentenced to death for heresy and burned at the stake at the Vieux-Marché in Rouen. She was posthumously exonerated in 1456, beatified in 1909 and canonised in

1920.

- ○ Her unusual actions both as a woman in charge of an army and as a military leader fighting a foreign occupier, added to her premature and unfortunate demise, made her a legendary heroine and a strong symbol of France in the 19th and 20th centuries.

INTRODUCTION

In 15th-century France, which was brutally divided, a young peasant girl who went by the name of Joan of Arc was motivated by the conviction that she had a divine mission. Through the strength of her will, she managed to get an audience with the future Charles VII, heir to a rather reduced Kingdom of France, in Chinon, and convinced him to entrust an army to her. Having become a military leader, she assumed leadership of the French troops and, on 8 May 1429, forced the English to lift their siege on Orléans, which led to her being called the Maid of Orléans.

The French army then won consecutive victories in Patay, Troyes, Châlons and, finally, Reims, in Burgundian territory. Joan thus enabled Charles to be crowned king of France in the Cathedral of Reims on 17 July 1429. However, after a few minor additional victories, the young woman ceased to be useful for the new king and, when she was captured by the Burgundian party on 23 May 1430, he did not pay her ransom. The Burgundians sold her to the English for £10 000. She was then handed over to Pierre Cauchon, the bishop of Beauvais, who brought a trial against her that took place between 21 February and 23 May 1431. Sentenced to death for heresy, she was burned at the stake at the Vieux-Marché in Rouen on 30 May.

Exonerated in 1456 by Pope Callixtus III (1378-1458), who declared her to be innocent, she was beatified by the Catholic Church in 1909 and eventually canonised in 1920. A medieval phenomenon, a feminist icon and the inspiration for an exaggerated form of nationalism, even today, Joan of Arc still fuels discussions and controversy.

BIOGRAPHY

JOAN, PEASANT GIRL AND PROPHET (1412 – FEBRUARY 1429)

While the Hundred Years' War (1337-1453) between the Kingdom of France and the Kingdom of England was still raging, Joan was born in Domrémy, a small village in the Duchy of Bar, on the eastern border of the kingdom. It was next to the Duchy of Lorraine, which at that time had been annexed to the Holy Roman Empire.

While her exact date of birth is unknown, most sources agree on the year 1412. She was the daughter of Jacques d'Arc, a landowner, and Isabelle Romée, who had five children together. Joan seemed like any other young girl her age: she was kind, cheerful and illiterate, and willingly undertook everyday tasks on her father's farm. She was particularly pious, and made a pilgrimage every Sunday to the Chapel of Bermont, in the neighbouring village of Greux.

At the age of 13, however, her enthusiasm for religion became even more pronounced. She even broke off the engagement that had been planned for her, after hearing heavenly voices. According to the young girl, Saint Catherine of Alexandria, Saint Margaret and Archangel Michael had entrusted two missions to her: freeing the Kingdom of France from the English occupiers, and delivering Charles VII to Reims so that he could be crowned king of France. At the age of 16, she revealed these mystical experiences to her cousin, Durand Lassois. He was confused and frightened and, without her parents' consent, took her to the commander of Vaucouleurs, Robert de Baudricourt (1400-1454). She asked him for a recommendation that would allow her to obtain an audience with Charles VII. This was an enormous request, and the young girl, undoubtedly considered to be a fanatic, was immediately sent back home.

Joan of Arc, painting by Pedro Américo, 1883.

When the English attacked the east of the Kingdom of France in 1428 and devastated Domrémy, her family fled to Neufchâteau, in the Duchy of Lorraine. However, in early 1429 she returned to Vaucouleurs. She was already the subject of enthusiastic public support for having counselled Charles II, duke of Lorraine (1364-1431). Robert de Baudricourt now took her seriously and even entrusted a small troop of fighters to her. Subsequently, she rode across Burgundian territory, disguised with short hair and men's clothes, towards the Loire Valley, to reach Charles VII's court in Chinon.

JOAN, INSPIRED MILITARY LEADER (MARCH 1429 – MAY 1430)

According to legend, once Joan had arrived in Chinon and been brought into the castle's great hall, she recognised the dauphin, who was disguised as one of his courtiers. In reality, when she arrived, on 23 February 1429, she had a private meeting with Charles and was only allowed before the court a few days later. We do not know what was discussed during their meeting. One thing is certain, however: the dauphin was changed by the meeting and convinced of Joan of Arc's good faith. She told him that Orléans would be freed, followed by Paris, that he would be crowned king in Reims, and that the Duke of Orléans, who had been imprisoned in England for 15 years, would soon be free. Instead of immediately trusting what the young woman had told him, the dauphin had her questioned by theologians in Poitiers, and Yolande of Aragon (1384-1442), his wife's mother, confirmed the girl's virginity. After an enquiry in

Domrémy, the dauphin and his advisers believed that this was a political opportunity not to be missed. If the public were enthusiastic and believed in the young girl, and the English were afraid of her as a missionary sent by God to help France, what risk could there be in sending her to battle? Charles therefore made her the head of a supply convey that assembled in Blois before setting off towards Orléans.

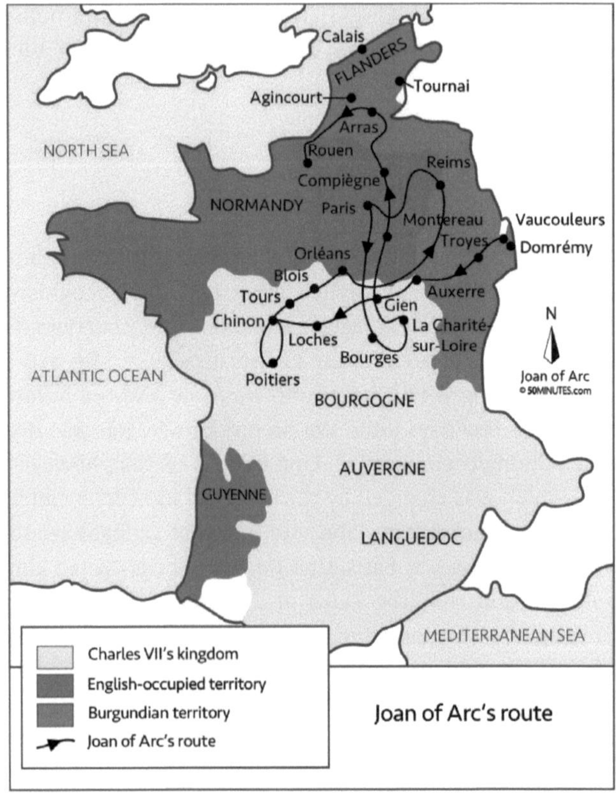

Joan of Arc's route

At that time, the Loire acted as the border between two territories: in the north, the land ruled by the English and their allies the Burgundians; in the south, the land ruled by the dauphin. The English wanted to take Orléans by any means possible, as the town would open the south to them. Consequently, in July 1428, they set up small forts and surrounded the town, whose people barricaded themselves in behind the town walls. As the siege seemed like it would last a while, a food supply ended up being necessary. Joan's convoy managed to trick the English garrisons and entered Orléans on 29 April 1429.

She handed out the abundance of food, which was met with considerable joy from the public. However, nothing was won, as the English were still set up all around the town. Joan therefore galvanised the troops, and thanks to their actions, the English forts, including Les Tourelles, which was south of the Loire, were seized one by one. The night between 7 and 8 May 1429, the English, who had suffered significant losses to their troops, were forced to lift the siege. Orléans was saved, and Joan earned her nickname of the Maid of Orléans.

She then left to go to the countryside of the Loire Valley and went to Loches. As her first mission had been a success, she now had to persuade the dauphin to go to Reims to be crowned king. However, the territories of Champagne were ruled by the Burgundians, who did not intend to let them pass. The French troops thus took Troyes, followed by Châlons and, finally, Reims. With Joan of Arc by his side, Charles VII was crowned king of France on 17 July 1429 in the cathedral in Reims. He was finally recognised as the legitimate sovereign.

With this task accomplished, Joan wanted to take back Paris, but Charles VII opposed this. An aborted attack ruled in his favour. There was not enough money and the mission was too risky. The army was therefore disbanded. The young woman, however, stuck to her instincts. She led her own small troop of mercenaries, which won several minor victories in the Loire Valley. She then decided to deliver aid to Compiègne, and made her way north. During the siege of the town, she was captured by a supporter of the Burgundians, John II of Luxembourg (1392-1441), on 23 May 1430. Her fate had just been turned on its head.

JOAN, EXPIATORY VICTIM (1431)

John II of Luxembourg, inconvenienced by his new prisoner, sold her to the English for £10 000. Charles VII did not send troops or ransom to save her. King Henry VI of England (1421-1471) wanted to be done with her and subjected her to the ecclesiastical justice system with one objective only: to get rid of her. As she had been captured in the diocese of Pierre Cauchon, the bishop of Beauvais, it was he who brought her to trial.

The trial lasted four months, from 21 February to 23 May 1431, with questioning and public indictments. Joan was mainly accused of heresy, sorcery and cross-dressing. However, the young girl responded with boldness and sense during the trial, which was transcribed in full. What followed had to happen behind closed doors, as tempers were starting to run high and the public supported her. In the cemetery in Rouen, a pretend stake was installed to terrorise her. She was frightened, and immediately signed, with a cross, her confession on a piece of parchment, but retracted this a few days later. Considered to have relapsed, meaning fallen back into her past mistakes, she was sentenced to death by being burned at the stake, with no possibility of an appeal. She died at the age of 19, suffering unbelievably, on 30 May 1431, at the Vieux-Marché in Rouen, and her ashes were thrown into the Seine.

Joan of Arc's trial

A copy of the trial in full, known as the 'd'Urfé manuscript', is still available, and is kept in the manuscript department of the National Library of France. It has been digitised and is now available in the digital library, Gallica. There are also three copies of the official statements, of which a sample is available at the library of the National Assembly in Paris.

It was not until 1456 that her trial was revised and her sentence declared invalid. But the legend of Joan was already spreading: she became the muse for defenders of the integrity of the kingdom, for ultra-Catholics, during the religious wars of the 16th century, and a romantic heroine in the historiography of the 19th century.

CONTEXT

FRANCE WITHOUT A KING

The late 14th and 15th centuries were particularly turbulent in France. King Charles VI (1368-1422) had, in fact, lost control of his mental faculties and gone crazy. Additionally, the regency council, presided over by Queen Isabeau of Bavaria (1371-1435), was split into two factions: the Armagnacs, led by Louis I of Orléans (1372-1407), the king's brother, and the Burgundians, led by Philip the Bold (1342-1404), the duke of Burgundy and the king's uncle. After the assassination of Louis I in 1407, the two sides ripped each other to shreds during a merciless civil war for power. King Henry V of England (1387-1422) took advantage of the situation and landed in Normandy in 1415. The Battle of Agincourt, which took place on 25 October, ended in a resounding victory for the English, as the French army had lost 6000 knights. This was a catastrophe for France.

The dauphin, Charles, met John the Fearless (1371-1419), son of Philip the Bold and the new duke of Burgundy, then the richest and most powerful province of the kingdom. The two men realised that they had to form an alliance against the English at all costs. But unfortunately, the Duke of Burgundy was assassinated, and his son Philip the Good (1396-1467), whose economic interests were better served by England, formed an alliance with Henry V. Backed into a corner, Queen Isabeau was forced to sign the Treaty of Troyes in 1420. This ensured the marriage of her daughter, Catherine of Valois (1401-1437) to the king of England, and the handing over of the French crown to him and to their descendants. Charles was thus deprived of his right to the throne.

In 1422, King Henry V of England and King Charles VI of France died in quick succession. King Henry VI of England was immediately recognised as the legitimate king of France by Burgundy, the Church and the University of Paris. The French capital welcomed him with open arms. The king's uncles were proclaimed regents, as the king himself was still a minor. One of them, the Duke of Bedford (1389-1435), moved to Paris and ensured regency for the continent.

France therefore no longer had a king, but had two uncrowned claimants: an English king, who was not recognised by the French nobility, other than in Burgundy, and the dauphin, Charles, son of the late king, whose legitimacy had been contested following a rumour. As he had little support and no more money, Charles withdrew to Bourges, which earned him the nickname King of Bourges. His situation was desperate and his chances of becoming the French sovereign seemed minimal, until Joan came along.

A TERRITORIAL IMBROGLIO

In 1429, the Kingdom of France was divided into three distinct territories: those governed by the English after the Battle of Agincourt, those ruled by their Burgundian allies, and finally those controlled by Charles.

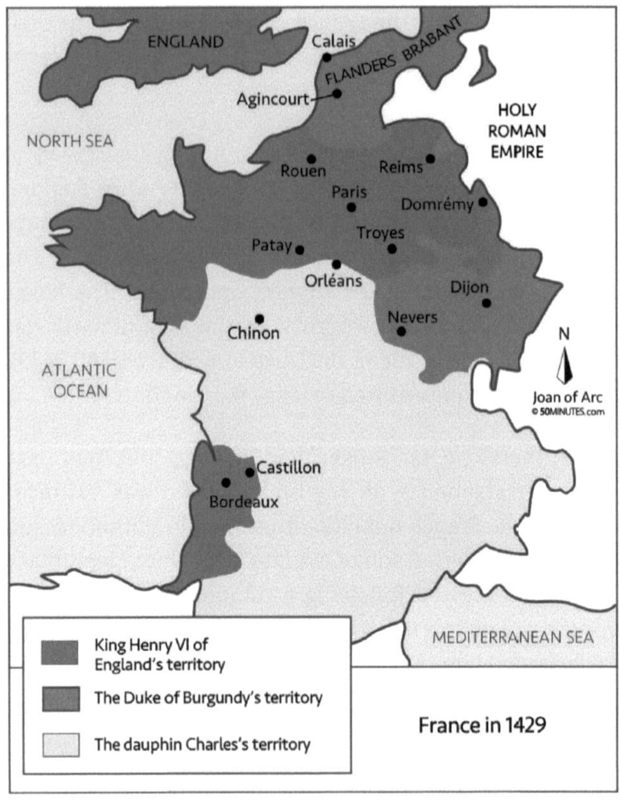

The English controlled a vast territory north of the Loire, which included Normandy, the Parisian area and Champagne, which acted as a northern border with Artois and a south-eastern border with Burgundy, controlled by their allies. In the east, the River Meuse acted as a border with the Holy Roman Empire, while in the west, Brittany remained neutral following the second Treaty of Guérande in 1381. These territories were complemented by the duchy of Guyenne, south of the River Charente, which had been held in its own right by the king of England since 1188.

The Burgundians, on the other hand, controlled a large territory which included the duchy and county of Burgundy, but also the counties of Boulogne, Artois, Flanders, Hainaut, Brabant and Holland, as well as the duchies of Lotharingia, Limburg and Luxemburg. They also occupied the duchies of Lorraine and Bar.

THE DUCHY OF BAR

The Duchy of Bar, where Joan of Arc's hometown was situated, was a sovereign entity at the time, part of which was under the rule of the Holy Roman Empire, and part of which, the *Barois mouvant*, was under the king of France, following homage paid in 1301. This territory, which was an immediate neighbour of the Duchy of Lorraine, was under the control of the Burgundians.

Finally, Charles controlled a vast territory in the south of the kingdom, which extended from the Loire to the Pyrenees and from Aunis to Dauphiné.

MAIDS AND PROPHETS

Throughout the Middle Ages, preachers and prophets poured forth: men, women and children. They delivered prophecies and willingly announced good news and catastrophes. They were systematically taken to religious authorities or universities, such as that of Paris, whose theology faculty had authority. In fact, only the Church was fully authorised to recognise prophets and confirm that they truly were who they claimed to be.

Women and young girls had to be maids, which meant unmarried and, above all, virgins. Indeed, only a virgin could bring a heavenly message. This is why Joan's virginity had to be duly confirmed twice, in March 1429 in Poitiers and in January 1431 in Rouen.

Other female prophets appeared at around the same time as Joan, such as Catherine de La Rochelle, whom Joan believed to be a liar, and Pieronne la Bretonne, who was also burned at the stake for heresy in Paris in 1430. Additionally, several women tried to imitate Joan of Arc after her death. One of them, Jeanne des Armoises, even convinced the town of Orléans to pay her a subsidy and fought between 1436 and 1439. Another, known as Jeanne de Sermaises, was imprisoned in 1458 and later freed. Both the English and the new king of France were terribly afraid of the appearance of a replacement Joan. The former therefore ensured that her corpse could not be the subject of worship for martyrdom, and the latter made sure that none of the other 'Joans' were ever officially recognised.

HIGHLIGHTS

THE SIEGE OF ORLÉANS

The towns of Angers and Orléans, on the Loire, were of significant strategic importance for the English. Capturing one of the two cities would enable them to gradually invade the southernmost territories, which were ruled by the dauphin. As Angers was very well defended, the English tried their luck with Orléans. In July 1428, they pillaged the villages between Paris and Orléans, and those around the latter. On 23 and 24 October, they seized the two forts on the south bank, Boulevard and Les Tourelles. The town was completely encircled. The inhabitants of Orléans were trapped: the suburbs were destroyed and their residents took refuge within the town walls.

The siege could now begin. The English built nine bastilles around the town in April 1429 and waited. Their objective was to make the siege last several months, until the reserves of water and food in Orléans ran out, which would force them to surrender. However, the supply convoy that accompanied Joan and her 500 soldiers set out from Blois on 28 April and made its way towards the town. While the young woman wanted to confront the English as soon as possible, the military leaders did not intend to do so, and the convoy approached the town without a fight. While the troops were occupying the English garrison of the Saint-Loup fort, boats sent from Orléans crossed the river and Joan boarded, along with the supplies and around 200 soldiers. She entered Orléans on 29 April and spent all of the following day handing out food to the local population.

A second convoy with reinforcements and additional troops set off at the beginning of May from Montargis and Gien. Joan left Orléans and went to personally inspect the English forts to establish her strategy. Once she had come up with a plan, she attacked them and seized them one after another. On 6 May, with the help of militia from the town, the fort at Les Augustins fell, and Joan suffered an injury to her foot. She was forbidden from taking part in the attacks on Boulevard and Les Tourelles the following day. On 7 May, however, she was back on her feet and joined her troops to seize the final forts. The French army, who wanted to be done with the forts, embarked on a pitched battle. Over 4000 of the 5000 English soldiers present at the beginning of the siege died, compared with only 2000 on the French side. The town could now be reached from the south once more, and William de la Pole (Duke of Suffolk, 1396-1450), who was in charge of the English, opted to save the rest of his army and lifted the siege.

Joan of Arc at the Siege of Orléans, painting by Jules Eugène Lenepveu, 1886-1890.

Orléans was saved and Joan's first mission was accompli-shed. The French troops then increased their advantage by recapturing towns such as Jargeau, Meung and Beaugency in mid-June, before their victory in Patay on 18 June, during which the English reinforcement troops that had come from

Paris were defeated.

Joan of Arc's military apparel

Joan of Arc wore to battle a suit of armour that the dauphin had had made in her size, as well as a sword decorated with five crosses, which was found buried in the church of Sainte-Catherine-de-Fierbois. She held a white standard or banner depicting Jesus with an angel on either side of him, and bearing the names of Jesus and Mary. She also had a triangular pennant with a depiction of an angel offering a lily to Mary. She had the appearance of a military leader and knew how to earn respect from those around her.

CHARLES VII'S CORONATION

In order to assert his legitimacy, the dauphin had to be crowned king of France. However, since 816, only the Archbishop of Reims had had the power to crown kings in the cathedral. But the route to Reims meant having to cross Champagne in the south, and the province was controlled by the Burgundians. The French army therefore avoided Auxerre, which belonged to the Duke of Burgundy, and arrived at the outskirts of Troyes, where Joan launched an attack. The inhabitants of Troyes surrendered, along with those of Châlons, thus allowing Joan and Charles VII to reach Reims in the evening of 16 July.

On 17 July 1429, Charles was crowned king of France by the

Archbishop of Reims, Renault de Chartres (1380-1444). He was first knighted by the Duke of Alençon the same morning, as he had not been yet. Then, at the beginning of the ceremony, he put on shoes adorned with fleurs-de-lys and golden spurs. He then swore an oath on the Bible to keep peace and to defend justice, the Church and the kingdom against all enemies. The Archbishop of Reims gave his ritual intercession and anointed the new king with the holy chrism contained in the holy vial. Then came the royal dubbing: the Grand Chamberlain Georges de la Trémoille (1384-1446) gave the monarch the coat adorned with fleurs-de-lys, the ring, the sceptre and the 'hand of justice'. The sword was handed over by the magnate Charles II of Albret (1407-1471). Finally, the archbishop anointed Charles atop his head, which concluded the official ceremony. He then solemnly placed a crown chosen from the cathedral's treasury especially for the occasion on his head, crowning him king of France. The new monarch could now finally sit on his throne while the peers came to pay him homage. The acclamation 'Vivat in aeturnum' ('May he have eternal life') resounded throughout the cathedral, as well as the sound of trumpets. During the ceremony, Joan of Arc remained by his side, carrying the standard.

Joan of Arc in Reims during Charles VII's coronation, painting by Jules Eugène Lenepveu, 1886.

The psychological effect of the coronation was significant: accusations of illegitimacy were forgotten, the Treaty of Troyes that disinherited him was nullified, and Charles was now the sole legitimate king of France. In Paris, the regent of France, the Duke of Bedford, catastrophically had Henry VI crowned in Notre-Dame Cathedral in Paris. However, he was not anointed by the holy vial, nor crowned according to the traditional rite. Propaganda was now set to work: Charles VII fought to recover his kingdom.

THE PEERS OF FRANCE

Traditionally, the 12 peers of France attended the coronation and held the crown above the head of the new king. They were the most powerful lords in the kingdom, and there were six secular peers and six ecclesiastical peers.

The secular peers were the dukes of Burgundy, Normandy and Guyenne, as well as the counts of Flanders, Toulouse and Champagne. However, when Charles VII was crowned, these titles were either vacant or held by the king's enemies. The great lords who were present for the occasion therefore carried out this role.

The ecclesiastical peers were the Archbishop of Reims and the bishops of Laon, Châlons, Langres, Noyon and Beauvais. Only the first three were present. As the other three were in Anglo-Burgundian territory, Charles invited Robert de Rouvres, bishop of Sées (died in 1453), Jean de Saint-Michel, bishop of Orléans (died in 1436 or 1438) and Jean Laiguisé, bishop of Troyes (died in 1450) to replace them.

THE TRIAL

Following her capture, Joan was imprisoned in the castle of Rouen where, despite difficult conditions, she was not tortured. Her trial began on 21 February 1431 and was held by an ecclesiastical tribunal whose members had been carefully selected by the Anglo-Burgundian party. Their mission was to find charges that would lead to a quick sentence. Pierre Cauchon, bishop of Beauvais, led the questioning. But Joan was honest and her answers were clear and consistent. In the end, ten charges were brought. Among other things, she was accused of being schismatic, an apostate, a blasphemer and a usurper. She was also judged for wearing men's clothes, which went against her natural condition. Finally, she was suspected of being inspired by demons' voices and of turning only to the judgement of God, and not that of the Church.

On 24 May, a stake was put up in Rouen cemetery in order to frighten the young girl. She was terrified and signed an agreement admitting her mistakes and surrendering herself to the Church. However, she renounced this a few days later and, out of free will or perhaps force, she donned men's clothes once more. The case was known in ecclesiastical tribunals: if someone who was accused of heresy returned to their past mistakes by retracting their confession, they were considered to have relapsed, which meant there was no way back. The punishment for this was being burned at the stake. On 30 May 1431, dressed once again in a dress made of heavy canvas, covered in sulphur, she was taken to the Vieux-Marché in Rouen, where a stake had been set up.

She was burned alive and died within minutes.

Joan of Arc's Death at the Stake, painting by Hermann Stilke, 1843.

The English, however, wanted to make sure that her remains could not under any circumstances be used for an outpouring of passion for relics or other acts of sorcery. Joan could not be a martyr for the French cause. Her remains were therefore once more covered in resin and burned for several hours before being thrown into the Seine. This marked the end of Joan of Arc's life story and the beginning of the myth.

TRIALS FOR WITCHCRAFT

Throughout the Middle Ages, witches were hunted across Europe. In 1326, a Papal bull from John XXII (c. 1244-1334) called for those who had turned away from the Christian faith in favour of demonic cults to be prosecuted. There were many trials of this kind from the 1420s onwards. For two centuries, the Inquisition hunted them. People who were slightly unusual, or simply those who had been reported by their neighbours, were tortured to get a confession from them before being burned at the stake. Two waves of witch hunting took place, from 1480 to 1520 and then from 1560 to 1650. It is thought that over 50 000 victims were thus sacrificed, mainly by ecclesiastical tribunals.

IMPACT

A NEW BALANCE OF POWER IN THE HUNDRED YEARS' WAR

Before Joan of Arc's arrival, the war was, on the whole, being won by the English. In fact, although their country was smaller and less densely populated, their conquests north of the Loire, supported by their solid base in the south-west, gave them an obvious lead in terms of men and resources, which they could mobilise quickly. Additionally, they had perfect knowledge of the terrain in the west of the country, which they had owned a century earlier. Finally, they had three undeniable psychological advantages: an army that had had the reputation of being invincible since 1415 with fearsome archers, the Treaty of Troyes which disinherited Charles VII, and their alliance with the Burgundians.

Joan of Arc undoubtedly influenced the course of the war, in many ways. Firstly, she had good strategical and military sense, which was recognised by other military leaders at the time and by her companions. In Orléans, she understood where to position artillery advantageously to cause the most damage to the English forts. In addition, she was an excellent leader and proved able to mobilise and galvanise her troops. Finally, when fighting the English, she allowed their weaknesses to be exposed, and she established Charles as the only legitimate king through his coronation.

She therefore enabled the tide to be turned in favour of the French and their new king. Only one significant ally was missing: Burgundy. After Joan's death, Charles VII and his successor continuously sought an alliance with Burgundy, through both diplomacy and violence, so that they would finally be done with this cumbersome vassal and with the English. The Hundred Year's War therefore ended without Joan, in 1453, with the Battle of Castillon and the reconquest of all the continental territories still under English control, apart from Calais, which was not recovered until 1558.

FROM THE DEATH SENTENCE TO CANONISATION

After Joan's sentencing and execution, her mother demanded that her trial be revisited. In 1450, Charles VII published an ordinance demanding that light be shone on this unjust sentence. Even then, his aims were political: he wanted to appease public opinion in Normandy, which he had just reconquered. The Catholic Church and the papacy, to whom Joan had, in vain, appealed during her trial, demanded that the trial be reopened in 1455. Pope Callixtus III (1378-1458) relied on the memory of the bishop of Lisieux, Thomas Basin (1412-1491), who described the inadequacies of the trial at length. Witnesses were called forward once again and, on 7 July 1456 in Rouen, the first trial was declared invalid and unfounded. Joan was exonerated. A cross was placed where her stake had been to honour the Maid.

It was not until the end of the 19th century, however, that the Church began proceedings to 'promote' Joan. The cause was begun in 1869 by the general prosecutor of Saint-Sulpice and supported by the bishop of Orléans, Mgr. Dupanloup (1802-

1878), who began to collect information in his diocese. Joan was first declared venerable on 27 January 1894, and a grand national ceremony was held in Notre-Dame Cathedral, Paris, to bless a replica of her banner. The enquiry in view of her beatification began three years later and ended in 1909. Three miraculous cures were duly witnessed in the dioceses of Arras, Évreux and Orléans. On 18 April 1909, Pope Pius X (1835-1914) beatified Joan of Arc. In 1910, proceedings to canonise her began. After new miracles and a quickly led investigation, Pope Benedict XV (1854-1922) declared her a saint in the Catholic Church on 16 May 1920, during a solemn mass in Saint Peter's Basilica in Rome. Her feast day was set as 30 May, the day of her death. Finally, on 2 March 1922, she was proclaimed a secondary patron saint of France.

STRONG SYMBOLISM

After the defeat of Sedan in 1870 and the annexation of Alsace and part of Lorraine by the German Empire, Joan became a strong symbol of occupied territory for France (the former Duchy of Bar was then part of Lorraine). The same year as her canonisation, on 14 July 1920, a law from the French Republic instigated a national feast day of Joan of Arc, a celebration of patriotism: Joan was to be celebrated every second Sunday in May. While the two feast days have now fallen out of use, celebrations of Joan are still organised every year in Orléans between 29 April and 8 May to celebrate the town's liberation by the Maid. Traditionally, the president or a member of the government goes there to officially represent the French Republic. Since 1998, anti-celebrations have also been organised, initiated by a social movement, aiming to oppose the religious and political nature of the festivities in Orléans.

Celebrations are also organised in Reims each year in early June, celebrating the triumphant arrival of Joan in Reims and the coronation of Charles VII in the cathedral.

Finally, Rouen is not to be outdone, with two significant places of remembrance. First of all, there is the Church of Saint Joan of Arc, constructed at the Vieux-Marché in 1979, which houses 13 stained-glass windows from the 16th century. A waxwork museum of Joan's life also opened its doors in 1953, although it closed down in 2012. In March 2015, a museum entirely dedicated to Joan of Arc's story was opened in Rouen. It was established in the former archbishop's house, where her sentence was pronounced in 1431 and her exoneration trial took place in 1456.

SUMMARY

1412
Joan of Arc is born

c. 1425
**Joan of Arc announces that
she can hear heavenly voices**

1429
23 Feb.: Joan of Arc meets the dauphin
Charles in Chinon
8 May: **Joan of Arc liberates Orléans,
where the English siege is lifted**
18 June: Joan of Arc wins another victory
in Patay
17 July: **Charles VII is crowned king
of France, at Joan's insistence**

1430
23 May: **Joan of Arc is captured in
Compiègne and sold to the English**

1430-1431
21 Feb. 1430–23 May 1431: A trial for witchcraft
begins

1431
30 May: **Joan is sentenced to death by being burned at the stake in Rouen**

1456
Joan of Arc is exonerated following a review of her trial

1909
Joan of Arc is beatified

1920
Joan of Arc is canonised

Joan of Arc © 50MINUTES.com

- When half of French territory was occupied by the English and their Burgundian allies, the dauphin Charles, heir of the late King Charles VI, was struggling to have his right to the throne recognised in France. However, there was a message of hope: Joan, a young girl from the east of the kingdom, had heard heavenly voices telling her that the English would soon be thrown out of France and that the dauphin would be crowned king in Reims.
- Charles wanted to believe this, and gave weapons to Joan

of Arc. She accompanied the supply convoy to Orléans, where the English had laid siege. She freed the town on 8 May 1429, which earned her the nickname of the Maid of Orléans. This victory was followed by various others that allowed the French to recover part of the Loire Valley.

- Fortified by this success, she crossed the territories in Champagne that were controlled by the Burgundians and reached Reims with the dauphin. On 17 July 1429, Charles was crowned king of France in the cathedral of Reims, rendering the claims of the young king of England to the throne obsolete. He was now the only legitimate king of France before God and his people.
- However, very soon, the new king's interest took priority over the recognition he owed to Joan: her army was disbanded and, when she was captured in Compiègne, he did not offer any ransom, nor did he send troops to find her. She was sold to the English by John II of Luxembourg.
- Joan was then brought before an ecclesiastical tribunal presided over by the bishop of Beauvais, Pierre Cauchon, in Norman territory, controlled by the English. A long trial for heresy ensued, which ended in a sentence: she was burned at the stake at the Vieux-Marché in Rouen on 30 May 1431. She was exonerated in 1456 by the Catholic Church, beatified in 1909 and canonised in 1920.
- She was highly symbolic throughout the 19th and 20th centuries, and her image is still closely associated with the French national identity. She is depicted as a heroine in contemporary historiography and is undoubtedly one of the best-known figures of European history from the Middle Ages.

We want to hear from you!
Leave a comment on your online library
and share your favourite books on social media!

FIND OUT MORE

BIBLIOGRAPHY

- Beaune, C. (2008) *Jeanne d'Arc : vérités et légendes*. Paris: Perrin.
- Boudet, J.-P. and Hélary, X. (2014) *Jeanne d'Arc : histoire et mythes*. Rennes: PUR.
- Bouzy, O. (1999) *Jeanne d'Arc : mythes et réalités*. La Ferté-Saint-Aubin: L'Atelier de l'Archer.
- Contamine, P. (1994) *De Jeanne d'Arc aux guerres d'Italie : figures, images et problèmes du XVe siècle*. Orléans, Paradigme.
- Duby, A. and Duby, G. (1974) *Les procès de Jeanne d'Arc*. Paris: Gallimard.
- Duparc, P. (1989) *Procès en nullité de la condamnation de Jeanne d'Arc*. Paris: Klincksieck.
- Pernoud, R. (1969) *La libération d'Orléans : 8 mai 1429*. Paris: Gallimard.
- Quicherat, J. (1849) *Procès de condamnation et de réhabilitation de Jeanne d'Arc, dite la Pucelle*. Paris: Jules Renouard et Cie.

ICONOGRAPHIC SOURCES

- *Joan of Arc*, painting by Pedro Américo, 1883. Royalty-free reproduction picture.
- *Joan of Arc at the Siege of Orléans*, painting by Jules Eugène Lenepveu, 1886-1890. Royalty-free reproduction picture.
- *Joan of Arc in Reims during Charles VII's coronation,*

painting by Jules Eugène Lenepveu, 1886. Royalty-free reproduction picture.

- *Joan of Arc's Death at the Stake*, painting by Hermann Stilke, 1843. Royalty-free reproduction picture.

50MINUTES.com

History

Business

Coaching

Book Review

Health & Wellbeing

IMPROVE YOUR GENERAL KNOWLEDGE
IN A BLINK OF AN EYE !

www.50minutes.com

© 50MINUTES.com, 2016. All rights reserved.

www.50minutes.com

Ebook EAN: 9782806297013

Paperback EAN: 9782806297020

Legal Deposit: D/2017/12603/245

Cover: © Primento

Digital conception by Primento, the digital partner of publishers.